Getting Born

BY RUSSELL FREEDMAN

drawings by Corbett Jones

Holiday House • New York

For Bella Halsted

Library of Congress Cataloging in Publication Data

Freedman, Russell.
Getting born.

SUMMARY: Describes the development and birth of
animals such as trout and turtles that hatch from eggs
and kittens and seahorses that are born alive.
1. Parturition—Juvenile literature.   2. Embryology
—Juvenile literature.   [1. Birth.   2. Embryology]
I. Jones, Corbett.   II. Title.
QP285.F73   596'.01'6   78-6673
ISBN 0-8234-0336-X

PHOTO CREDITS: Pages 3, 6–7, 12, 14–17, Jane Burton from Bruce Coleman, Inc.; 9, Alan Blank from Bruce Coleman, Inc.; 10, photo by Lilo Hess;
19–23, 25, New York Zoological Society; 24, Oswald J. Rapp from National
Audubon Society/PR; 1, 26, 29, Richard Frear from National Audubon So-
ciety/PR; 31, 33, Martin Iger from Globe Photos; 34–35, Richard Hewett
from Globe Photos; 36–40, from *Birth of a Foal* by Jane Miller, copyright ©
1977 by Jane Miller, reproduced by permission of J. B. Lippincott Company.

Brown Trout eggs, greatly enlarged

These eggs are almost ready to hatch. They lie hidden in a bed of gravel at the bottom of a swift stream. Those dark spots are the bulging eyes of baby trout, about to be born.

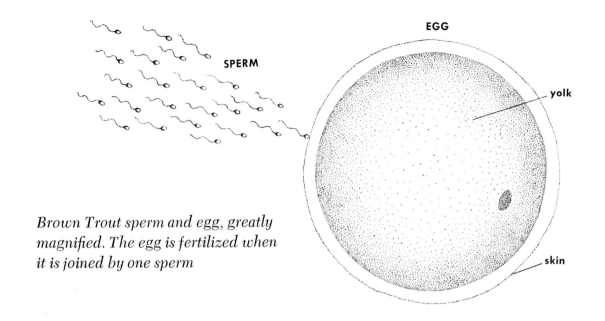

EGG

SPERM

yolk

skin

Brown Trout sperm and egg, greatly magnified. The egg is fertilized when it is joined by one sperm

How does a pea-sized trout egg grow into a baby trout? How does any egg become a baby animal? An egg cannot grow into an animal by itself. First, the egg must be fertilized (fur-TUH-lized). It must be joined by a sperm from the father.

A sperm is a tiny living cell, smaller than the eye can see. Under a microscope, it looks like a wriggling tadpole. Millions of sperm cells come from the father's body.

An egg, called an ovum (OH-vum), is a living cell from the mother. It is much bigger than a sperm because it is packed with lots of egg yolk, or food.

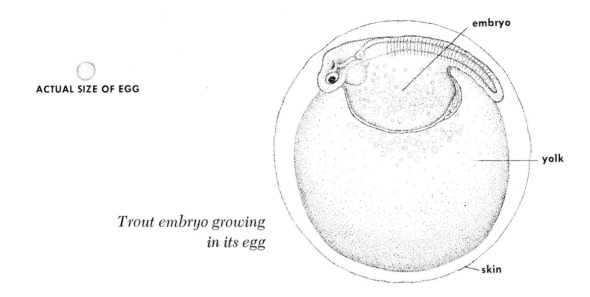

ACTUAL SIZE OF EGG

embryo

yolk

skin

*Trout embryo growing
in its egg*

Trout eggs are fertilized in the water. As the female trout lays her eggs, a male sheds his sperm. The father's sperm race through the water toward the mother's eggs. Only one sperm can enter an egg. It passes through a special opening in the egg's skin. When a sperm cell joins with an egg cell, a new life begins to grow.

A fertilized egg holds a living creature called an embryo (em-BREE-oh), which means "growing within." As a trout embryo grows, it gets all its food from the rich yellow yolk of its egg.

The trout hatching here has been growing in its egg for forty days. Just before hatching, it began to wriggle and squirm. Its tail broke through the egg's skin. Now the tail is being pulled out straight by the rushing current of the stream.

These newly hatched trout have no scales, no fins, and no mouths. They leave the eggs with big balls of yolk still attached to their bellies. Each hatchling has enough yolk to last until its mouth opens.

At first, the babies are too weak to swim. They stay close to their nest, hiding among the gravel. As they grow bigger, their yolk sacs shrink. When they have used up all their yolk, they are strong enough to swim into the stream and start feeding themselves. Baby fish are often called "fry."

Some fish, like the molly shown here, keep their eggs inside their bodies. A molly's eggs are fertilized when the father's sperm enter the mother's body. As the embryos grow, they lie curled up head to tail within their mother. Each embryo gets food from a yolk sac attached to its belly. When it has used up all its egg yolk, it is ready to be born.

At birth, a baby molly slides out of its mother's body. It enters the water as a fully formed young fish, strong enough to swim and feed by itself.

Guppies, swordtails, and some sharks also give birth to live young.

Molly giving birth

A mother seahorse lays her eggs in a pouch on the father's belly. The eggs are fertilized as they drop into the soft, spongy lining of the pouch, where the embryos start to grow. Each embryo gets some food from its egg yolk and some from its father. Food flows from the father to the embryo through tiny blood vessels in his pouch.

As the embryos get bigger, their father's pouch swells like a balloon. When he is ready to give birth, he coils his long tail around some seaweed. He bends backward and forward, trying to squeeze the babies out. Each time he bends, a young seahorse is shot into the water. As many as two hundred babies may come popping out of the pouch before it is empty. They swim off in all directions, and their father never sees them again.

Male seahorse giving birth

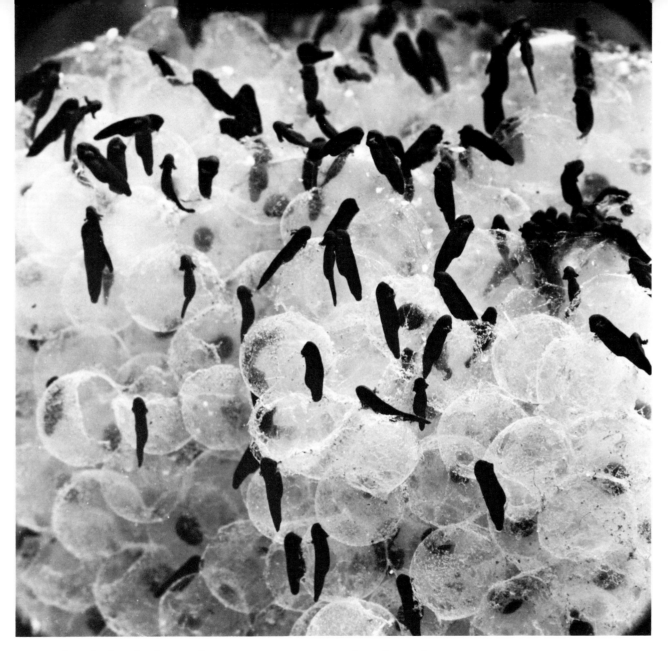

Newly hatched tadpoles of the Common Frog, greatly enlarged

Frogs lay their jelly-covered eggs in quiet pools and ponds. As the eggs leave the mother frog's body, they are fertilized by the father's sperm. Soon, you can see small dark tadpoles squirming inside the eggs.

A batch of eggs about to hatch seems to bubble and boil with motion. Now the egg jelly begins to melt. This makes it easier for the tadpoles to escape from their eggs and wriggle into the pond.

Some of the tadpoles shown here are just hatching. Others are clinging to empty balls of egg jelly. They hang on with tiny suction cups on their chins. The tadpoles are about ¼ inch (roughly ⅝ centimeter) long. Gills for breathing are growing from the sides of their heads. They do not yet have eyes or mouths. For the next two or three days, until their mouths open, they will feed on leftover yolk from their eggs. The yolk is stored inside their fat bellies.

At first the tadpoles hang quietly from egg jelly or plants. If anything disturbs them, they twitch their tails and swim a short distance. In this picture, you can see their long feathery gills. Their tails are growing longer too. Their lidless eyes and small round mouths are just beginning to show. When their mouths open, the tadpoles will start to explore their pond.

Gilled tadpoles, 2–3 days old

gills

As the tadpoles get bigger, a fold of skin grows over their gills. The gills disappear inside their heads. The tadpoles begin to breathe as fish do, by sucking water into their mouths. Their bodies become plump and speckled with silvery dots. Their long tails look like flowing, waving fans. By now, the tadpoles are strong swimmers. They spend their days nibbling at plants and darting away from enemies. Three weeks after hatching, they are about an inch (roughly 2½ centimeters) long.

Tadpoles feeding on pondweed, 2–3 weeks old

*Seven-week-old tadpole
with hind legs growing*

About seven weeks after hatching, a Common Frog tadpole begins to change again. Tiny stumps break through the skin just above its tail. The stumps grow longer and become strong legs. Then the front legs begin to grow. Now the tadpole is going through a metamorphosis (MET-uh-MOR-fuh-sis), which means "change in form." It is changing from a tadpole to a frog. Its small round mouth widens into a frog's mouth. Its beady eyes become bulging frog's eyes. Its skin gets thicker and tougher.

*Ten-week-old tadpole
with tail almost absorbed*

Other changes are taking place inside the tadpole's body. Its fish-like gills disappear. In place of gills, the tadpole grows lungs for breathing air. Meanwhile, it stops eating plants. As it changes from a plant-eating tadpole to a meat-eating frog, it cannot feed itself. Instead, it gets food by absorbing its own tail. Every day its tail shrinks. About ten weeks after hatching, the tadpole has become a froglet with just a stump of a tail. It keeps sticking its head out of the water to test its lungs. Soon it will start hopping about on land.

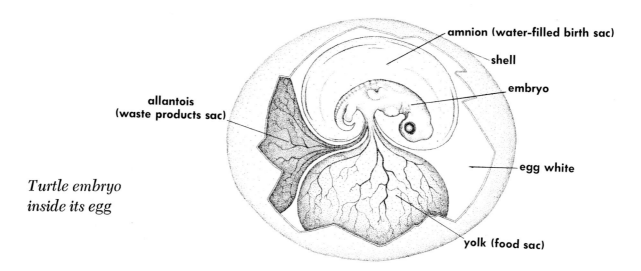

amnion (water-filled birth sac)

shell

embryo

allantois
(waste products sac)

egg white

*Turtle embryo
inside its egg*

yolk (food sac)

The eggs of reptiles and birds are different from those of fishes and frogs. Reptiles and birds lay their eggs on land. The eggs are fertilized by the father while they are still inside the mother. A hard shell grows around each egg before it leaves the mother's body.

At the center of a reptile or bird egg, an embryo floats gently in a pool of water. It lies curled up in a rubbery sac called the amnion (am-NEE-ahn). This sac is filled with special waters that bathe the embryo and cushion it from bumps. Another sac holds the egg's yolk. A third sac, called the allantois (uh-LAN-toh-is), is a storage place for the embryo's waste products. The rest of the egg is filled with egg white, which holds water and some extra food.

As a reptile or bird grows in its egg, it uses up most of its egg yolk and white. By the time it is ready to hatch, it barely fits inside the egg. Before it can escape, it must tear open its rubbery amnion, or birth sac. Then it must crack the hard shell that surrounds it.

All reptiles and birds are born with a sharp tool called an "egg tooth," which helps them cut their way into the world. The Box Turtle hatching in this picture has a pointed egg tooth at the tip of its snout. After the turtle hatches, the egg tooth is no longer needed. In a few days, it falls off.

Box Turtle hatching

egg tooth

Turtles hide their hard-shelled eggs. They always bury them in the ground. A Box Turtle lays four or five eggs at a time. The babies hatch in about three months and scramble out of their underground nest. The egg shown here was removed from its nest so it could be photographed as it hatched. It would fit easily into a teaspoon.

Even with its sharp egg tooth, a turtle must struggle for hours to escape from its egg. It chips away at the shell until it cracks a hole big enough to stick its head through. Then it thrashes about until the shell splits all the way open. Blinking its eyes, the baby turtle crawls out. It enters the world wet from the special waters of its birth sac, which has protected it until now.

Snakes lay eggs with leathery shells that stretch and bend. The eggs in this picture were laid by an Indian Rock Python, a giant snake that may be 20 feet (roughly 6 meters) long or more. The eggs are big too. Each egg is about 5 inches (roughly 12½ centimeters) long. A mother python coils her body around her eggs and warms them like a brooding hen. She guards the eggs for two months, until they are ready to hatch.

When a baby python hatches, it twists its head from side to side. The sharp egg tooth on its snout slashes through the leathery eggshell. The python hatching here has already made several slits in its egg. It keeps pushing its head in and out, as though it is testing the air.

Indian Rock Python hatching

Several hours pass before the python cuts a big enough hole to slither out of its egg. At birth, the hatchling is about 2 feet (roughly ½ meter) long. It was able to fit into its egg only because it was coiled up tightly. When it dries off, it will start hunting for its first meal.

Not all snakes lay eggs. A baby garter snake grows from a fertilized egg inside its mother's body, where it is wrapped in a water-filled birth sac. By the time the snake is big enough to be born, its birth sac is stretched tightly around it.

The baby garter snake shown below has just slipped out of its mother's body. It slides into the world like a package wrapped in cellophane. In a moment, when it starts moving, it will break out of its birth sac.

Common Garter Snake in its birth sac

One after another, baby snakes keep sliding out of the mother snake's body. Every so often she pauses to rest, as though she has finished giving birth. Then she delivers another batch of babies wrapped in sacs. This mother gave birth to fifty-seven babies in about two hours. Soon she will leave them to take care of themselves, as all mother snakes do. Rattlesnakes and copperheads also give birth to living young.

Mother garter snake with newborn young

Domestic chicken hatching

A chicken grows inside its egg for twenty-one days. A day or two before hatching, the cramped and crowded chick pokes its beak through its rubbery birth sac. It starts pecking at the eggshell with the egg tooth at the tip of its beak. Special hatching muscles in back of its neck give it enough power to hammer hard. The chick pecks, then sleeps, then pecks some more. Nothing seems to happen at first, but with every peck the shell gets weaker. After thousands of pecks, the chick's beak breaks through the shell.

That first small hole is just the beginning of the chick's work. Peeping loudly, it twists its head from side to side, trying to twist off its clinging birth sac. More of the eggshell chips away, and the hole gets bigger. The chick also tries to stretch out its body. It braces its feet against the wall of the egg and pushes as hard as it can. For hours the chick twists and squirms, pushes and heaves, stopping to nap in between. Finally, cracks start to zigzag across the middle of the egg.

The chick has just enough strength left to finish hatching. More pushing and heaving and squirming, and the egg gradually splits in half. The chick is still curled up tightly, as it has been all along. Its wet, downy feathers cling to its body. Slowly, it begins to wriggle out of the broken egg. Six hours have passed since the chick made that first small hole in the shell.

Kicking its big feet, the chick flops out. At last it can stretch its body. Soon it will try to stand up, but its legs are too weak and wobbly to carry it very far. Right now, it must be kept warm by its mother, or in an incubator (IN-kyuh-BAY-tur), until its feathers dry. It has enough leftover yolk tucked into its belly to last a day or two. After that, the chick will be strong enough to run around and peck for food on the ground.

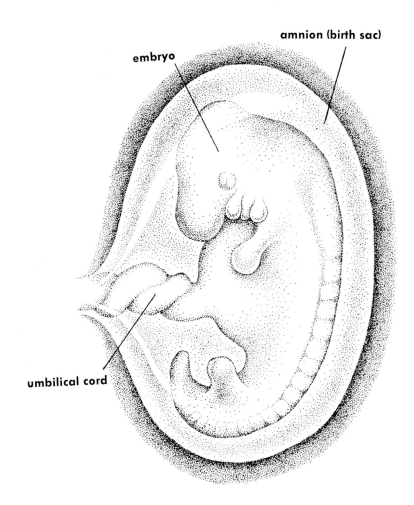

embryo

amnion (birth sac)

umbilical cord

Mammal embryo

Animals that nurse their young with mother's milk are called mammals. Cats are mammals. So are dogs and horses, dolphins and elephants. Humans are mammals too.

Like other animals, mammals come from fertilized eggs. A mother mammal keeps her eggs inside her body. Each embryo grows in its mother's uterus (YOO-tur-us), where it is protected by a water-filled birth sac. The sac acts as a shock absorber when the mother runs or leaps or falls. The embryo gets food and oxygen from its mother through a long tube called the umbilical (um-BILL-uh-kul) cord.

Birth of a kitten

If you put your hand on a mother cat's belly before she gives birth, you can feel her kittens moving inside her. Kittens spend nine weeks growing in their mother's uterus. When they are ready to be born, muscles that have held the uterus tightly shut begin to relax. Other muscles in the mother's body start to push the first kitten out. Little by little, it gets pushed into its mother's birth canal. The walls of the birth canal stretch as the kitten slides through on its birth journey.

Here you can see the head of a kitten, wrapped in its birth sac, slipping out of its mother's body.

Before the first kitten is even dry, another one is on the way. As each kitten is born, the mother bites off its birth sac. She licks the blind, helpless kitten with her rough tongue, cleaning its eyes, its nose and its matted fur. Although the mother is a house cat, she eats the birth sac as a wild cat does. Otherwise it will decay and cause an odor that might attract enemies. She also bites off the umbilical cord and eats that. A kitten's belly button, or navel, marks the spot where it was once attached by a cord to its mother.

Newborn kittens need warmth and milk. They spend most of their time cuddled against their mother's body, nursing and sleeping, until their eyes open and their legs are strong enough to carry them around.

Biting off the birth sac

Most mammals are born headfirst. Dolphins enter the world the other way around. A dolphin calf is born underwater. As soon as its head leaves its mother's body, it must swim to the surface for air. Otherwise it will drown.

The calf grows in its mother's uterus for about a year. Its birth may take half an hour or more as the mother stretches and strains to push the calf out. First, its limp little tail appears. Waving back and forth in the water, the tail slides slowly out of the mother's body. When the calf is about half-way out, the mother gives a mighty heave. The calf slips into the water, where it dangles from its long umbilical cord.

Underwater birth of a dolphin

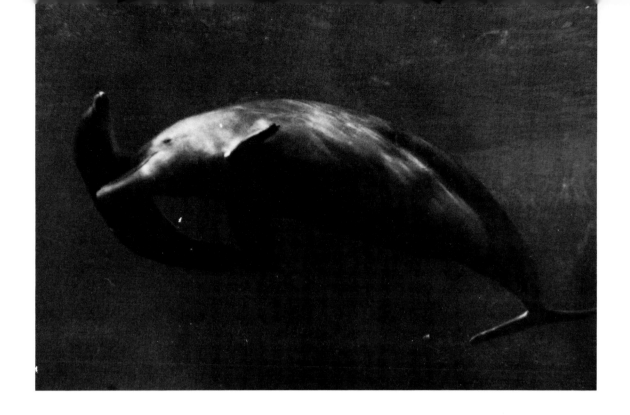

A moment after giving birth, the mother dolphin whirls around. As she twists her body, she breaks the umbilical cord. Now the calf must rise to the surface, where it can breathe. The mother takes no chances. She dives beneath her baby, ready to push it up with her strong beak.

Usually the calf needs no help. It swims up by itself, opens its blowhole and sucks in its first breath of air. Then it splashes back into the water and swims by its mother's side.

Birth of a Welsh Mountain pony

The foal being born here has been growing in its mother's uterus for eleven months. Shortly before this picture was taken, the mother was cantering around a field. When she felt her muscles working and the foal moving inside her, she found a quiet place where she could lie down. The foal has just started to come out. Its front legs have already broken through its thin birth sac.

In a few minutes, the foal is all the way out. Its hair is wet and matted from the waters of its birth sac, which still clings to it. Its eyes are closed, but they will open in a moment. Now, its mother lifts her head and looks around. She reaches over to nuzzle the foal. She will keep sniffing it for an hour or so, learning to recognize her foal by its own special smell.

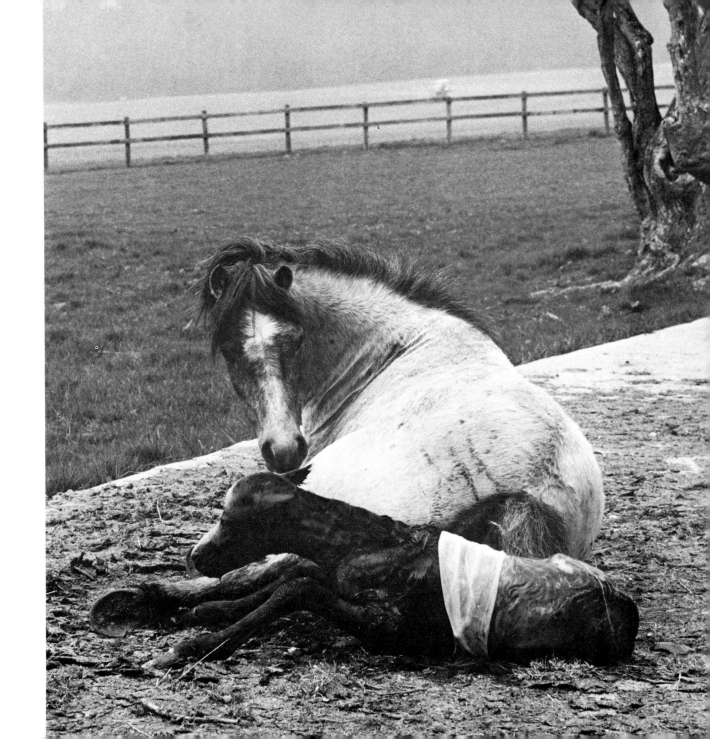

The foal is still joined to its mother by its umbilical cord, but it is already trying to stand up. At first it is too weak to stand. Its spindly legs wobble and collapse, and it falls down. But it keeps trying. As the foal struggles to rise, it breaks the umbilical cord and pulls itself out of the birth sac. By the time it is fifteen minutes old, it can stand by itself.

The mother cleans the foal with her tongue and nuzzles it
against her warm body. The morning air helps dry its wet
hair. Soon the foal is able to follow its mother to a nearby
field. It is still unsteady on its legs, and it sways as it walks,
but its legs are getting stronger with every step. When the
foal discovers its mother's milk-filled udder, it begins to nurse.
It will need her milk for the next six months.